Bootstrap

Beginners

Quick and easy design for web and app programmer

Bootstrap 4 – For Beginners by
Marcelo Carlos Cancinos

ISBN: 9798649655231

Imprint: Independently published

Content

What is Bootstrap?

It is the most popular CSS Framework. Framework is understood as a working environment, a set of practices and criteria to focus on a particular problem. While CSS (Cascading Style Sheets) is a graphic design language, for HTML document styles or markup language.

No prior knowledge of Bootstrap is required, but a little html, css and javascript.

Bootstrap is Open Source, which means it is open source and free. It allows the creation of beautiful designs in very short development times. Adaptable to different browsers and devices since it is multiplatform, responsive interfaces and adaptive design. And also Mobile First, allowing you to create a version optimized for mobile devices and then expand to the web. Since bootstrap not only allows the design of applications but also favors web design, and streamlines the stylization of the user interface, that is, the part with which the user interacts

.

One of the advantages of Bootstrap is that due to its great agility and speed when designing, it is possible to create prototypes, that is, to generate a prototype of a product very quickly, with an agile, adaptable and pleasant design, easy to modify.

We can summarize by saying that Bootstrap is a library or set of css styles and being a popular freamework on the web, you often find many templates and example codes or javascript plugins for animations or behaviors, it is also robust since it is found all the time under review and development.

How to use:

Basically there are two ways to start using Bootstrap. The first is through the CDN and the second is by downloading it. Either a direct download from the site or through package managers such as npm, bower, yarn.

CDN (Content Delivery Network) / Download:

The cdn is the easiest way to use bootstrap, since you just have to copy a web address into our html file. Although this is the fastest way, when using cdn, every time our website is loaded, the css and js files from the bootstrap server will be read. The advantage of this, which at the same time is a disadvantage, is that if bootstrap makes a modification to its code, this will directly affect our website or app. Whereas if we opt for the option of downloading bootstrap on our server, nobody, only us, will modify said code or css files. And therefore it allows us more flexibility to download the code at the time of design, since we can modify the code, styles and bootstrap behaviors at our whim.

To start:

Let's start by saying that the official Bootstrap site is **getbootstra.com**, here we can find examples, tutorials, topics, documentation and information on how to use the cdn and download links, either direct download or through package managers.

We will also find a Premium area for users who need more professional designs predesigned with new plugins, components, documentation and construction tools..

For the latter, we can enter **themes.getbootstrap.com** and acquire the theme that suits your tastes and needs, for an approximate cost of $ 49.00 also, remember that bootstrap is a free tool and that is where we will dedicate ourselves.

It is also worth clarifying that, apart from the official bootstrap themes site, there are many unofficial sites, including some with free themes, but Bootstrap is no longer responsible for the erroneous or malicious code that may arise from the modification of what was developed by the company.

Download:

In the download link of the official bootstrap site we can find different ways to use it.

Css y Js compiled:

Bootstrap files are downloaded here. And these, together with the files of our project, would be ready to be uploaded to a server and used.

Source Files:

It is similar to the previous option, but Bootstrap development sources are also downloaded along with some other tools.

Cdn Bootstrap:

Just by copying the links in our file **html** It's enough. It is recommended that the link **<link>** we place it in our area **<head>** as we see in the example below and that the **<script>** let's locate them at the end of the block **<body>**, since the java scripts take a little longer to load and it is convenient that our website begins to see immediately with their css styles to have a good design and finally we will have time to load the java scripts that will give us the appropriate behavior.

```
<!DOCTYPE html>
        <html lang="eN" dir="ltr">
         <head>
          <meta charset="utf-8">
          <title>Web Test</title>
          <link rel="stylesheet"
        href="https://stackpath ... >
          </head>
          <body>
            <h1>This is a test</h1>

    <script src="https://code.jquery.com/ ... ></script>
    <script src="https://cdnjs.cloudflare.com/ajax/ ...
></script>
    <script src="https://stackpath.bootstrapcdn.com/ ...
></script>


    </body>
</html>
```

In this example the code of the links and the scripts was summarized for didactic questions of space. To obtain the complete code it is recommended to enter the download area of the official bootstrap site.

Package Manager:

It is similar to downloading bootstrap as the second option, but it is useful if we use it in NodeJs, Ruby, .NET, .php.
These use the Package Managers of their systems as npm in **NodeJs**.
The different ways to use these package managers are on the Bootstrap website. So here I will just put the NodeJs **npm** example.

$ npm install bootstrap

We will see its use within a NodeJs work environment in an example later.

typography:
A good way to start learning bootstrap is by looking at their design styles, and for that it is essential to start with fonts.
As we saw bootstrap redefines the style that comes by default in the browser and makes it compatible for a style that is seen in one way in one browser to look the same way in a different browser or on a different device. Let's explain this with an example. Internet Explorer has its default fonts, for example for a **<h1>** tag, while for the same Google Chrome tag it could have another font or another size. The same thing happens if we see our website on a laptop or mobile phone..

Well bootstrap solves this by setting the same font and font size for all browsers and devices for its different classes. So if we use a class **class="h1"** or a **<h1>** We should see it the same way on different devices and / or browsers. That's why I think it's good to start with the fonts in this book. In this way we can see how our content will look.

Let's see what these styles would look like in headings.

Headings:

Remember that the html tags of headings, go from **<h1>** to **<h6>,** in *Image 1,* we can appreciate how they would look.

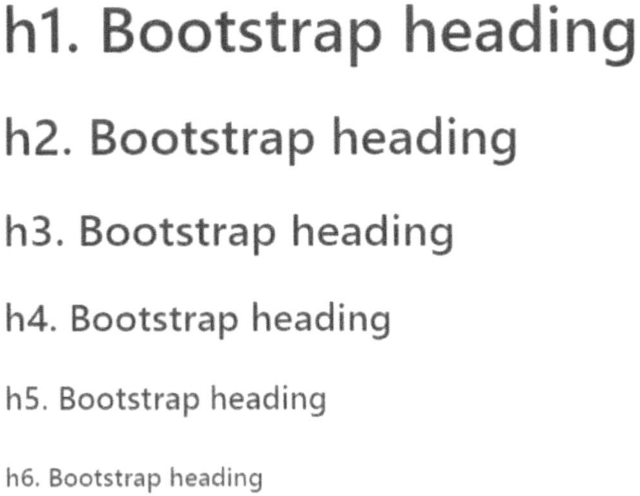

h1. Bootstrap heading

h2. Bootstrap heading

h3. Bootstrap heading

h4. Bootstrap heading

h5. Bootstrap heading

h6. Bootstrap heading

Image 1

To achieve this result, it is possible to do it in the conventional way that is using **<h>** type labels.

<h1>h1. Bootstrap heading</h1>

<h2>h2. Bootstrap heading</h2>

<h3>h3. Bootstrap heading</h3>

<h4>h4. Bootstrap heading</h4>

<h5>h5. Bootstrap heading</h5>

<h6>h6. Bootstrap heading</h6>

Or we can also use any type of tag, such as a **<p>** type paragraph tag and tell it to use the bootrstrap class that has a particular style, for example a **h1** type. In this way, let's see an example of how to achieve the same result as in image 1, using **<p>** type tags this time.

```
<p class="h1">h1. Bootstrap heading</p>

<p class="h2">h2. Bootstrap heading</p>

<p class="h3">h3. Bootstrap heading</p>

<p class="h4">h4. Bootstrap heading</p>

<p class="h5">h5. Bootstrap heading</p>

<p class="h6">h6. Bootstrap heading</p>
```

Let's see another example with a **\<h3\>** header, but this time we will use the **\<small\>** tag to remind us, this tag reduces the text a little with respect to the size it uses. But it will not be the result of small that interests us, but the class that we will put inside that will be a **class = "text-muted"** that will give us the sensation of visual silence or rather a decrease or saturation of the text. It is best explained by seeing *Image 2*.

Fancy display heading With faded secondary text

Image 2

Let's see the necessary code to generate this example.

```
<h3>
Fancy display heading
<small class="text-muted">With faded secondary
text</small>
</h3>
```

All these examples can be found by accessing the bootstrap website at the following link: https://getbootstrap.com/docs/4.3/content/typography/

Display headers:

The bootstrap site tells us that conventional headers, that is, those with a <h> type tag, allow us to have a design on our site or standard format application, but if we want headers of a larger size, they provide us with their **display headers**. , let's see *Image 3* where they are appreciated and then a code example of how to generate said effect.

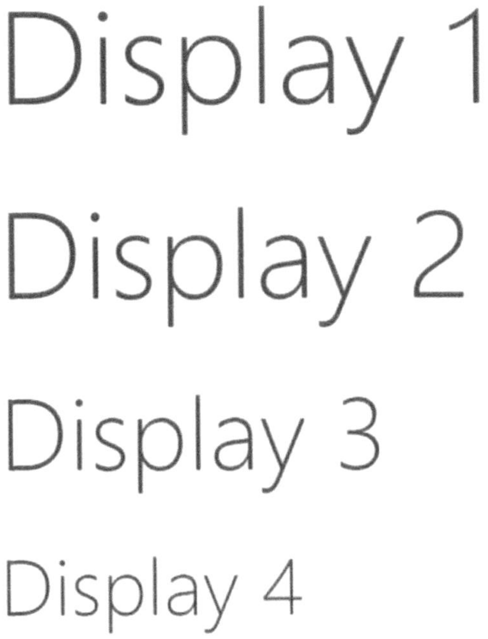

Display 1

Display 2

Display 3

Display 4

Image 3

```
<h1 class="display-1">Display 1</h1>
<h1 class="display-2">Display 2</h1>
<h1 class="display-3">Display 3</h1>
<h1 class="display-4">Display 4</h1>
```

Lead class:

Now let's look at the example of a paragraph with a font used in the lead class.

Vivamus sagittis lacus vel augue laoreet rutrum faucibus dolor auctor. Duis mollis, est non commodo luctus.

Image 4

```
<p class="lead">
```
Vivamus sagittis lacus vel augue laoreet rutrum dolor auctor. Dios mollis, est non commodo luctus.
```
</p>
```

Text Styles:

Here in *Image 5*, it is easy to see the example and as until now we will see below the code necessary to generate it.

You can use the mark tag to highlight text.

This line of text is meant to be treated as deleted text.

This line of text is meant to be treated as no longer accurate.

This line of text is meant to be treated as an addition to the document.

This line of text will render as underlined

This line of text is meant to be treated as fine print.

This line rendered as bold text.

This line rendered as italicized text.

Image 5

```
<p>You can use the mark tag to
<mark>highlight</mark> text.</p>
<p><del>This line of text is meant to be treated as
deleted text.</del></p>
<p><s>This line of text is meant to be treated as no
longer accurate.</s></p>
<p><ins>This line of text is meant to be treated as an
addition to the document.</ins></p>
<p><del>This line of text is meant to be treated as
deleted text.</del></p>
<p><u>This line of text will render as
underlined.</u></p>
<p><small>This line of text is meant to be treated as
fine print.</small></p>
<p><strong>This line rendered as bold
text.</strong></p>
<p><em>This line rendered as italicized
text.</em></p>
```

Alignment:

Let's see the different options to align the **blockquote**.

```
<blockquote class="blockquote">
  <p class="mb-0">Vivamus sagittis lacus vel augue
laoreet rutrum dolor auctor. Dios mollis, est non
commodo luctus.
  </p>
</blockquote>
```

In this example above we can see how to use the blockquote class without alignment and we have put a paragraph mark inside. For those who do not know, the blockquote brand is often used to insert texts that refer to external sites or notes. Therefore it is very common to add a footer maca inside these bockquote blocks. Let's see an example with the **<cite>** mark but we will use the blockquote-footer style for the blockquote

```
<blockquote class="blockquote">
  <p class="mb-0">Vivamus sagittis lacus vel augue
laoreet rutrum dolor auctor. Dios mollis, est non
commodo luctus.
  <footer class="blockquote-footer">Someone famous
in <cite title="Source Title"lSoruce
Title</cite></footer>
  </p>
</blockquote>
```

The blockquote class has a left alignment by default,
but we can give it a right or centered one.

```
<blockquote class="blockquote text-center">
```

```
<blockquote class="blockquote text-right">
```

Finally in this part of the bootstrap website we talk
about the lists.

But not only blockquotes can be aligned, but also other
html marks like paragraph marks <p>, let's see
alignments, left, right, center and justified.

```
<p class="text-left">Texto de Prueba</p>
```

```
<p class="text-right">Texto de Prueba</p>
```

```
<p class="text-center">Texto de Prueba</p>

<p class="text-justify">Texto de Prueba</p>
```

Adaptive Alignment:
Depending on the screen size of the device, the texts can change their alignment, let's see what these screen sizes are.

SM (small)
MD (Medium)
LG (Large)
XL (Xtra Large)

What will happen is that for different types of devices or better said screen sizes, we can have different alignments, let's go an example.

```
<p class="text-sm-right"> Sample text </p>
<p class="text-md-left"> Sample text </p>
<p class="text-lg-center"> Sample text </p>
```

In this way for **small** screens, our **Sample text** will be aligned to the right. If you change the size of the screen, either because you change the size of the browser or rotate the screen of the cell phone or change the resolution of the screen or change the device to a medium size, then the **Sample text** will be seen on the left according to our example and to the center for a big screen.

For the case only the alignment will be used without indicating the size of the screen, then for any size that will be our alignment.
We can also do a vertical alignment.

baseline top middle bottom text-top text-bottom

Image 6

```
<span class="align-baseline">baseline</span>
<span class="align-top">top</span>
<span class="align-middle">middle</span>
<span class="align-bottom">bottom</span>
<span class="align-text-top">text-top</span>
<span class="align-text_bottom">text-bottom</span>
```

Fixed:

The fixed class is used to generate a kind of object or group of objects that will be fixed on the screen in a specific position.

One option is for example to set the text at the top, so if you continue to scroll down with the scroll bar we will see that the fixed text remains at the top.

```
<h1 class="fixed-top"> Fixed text </h1>
```

The other example that may interest us is to set a text, but this time at the bottom of the screen. This would be done as follows:

```
<h1 class="fixed-bottom"> Fixed text </h1>
```

In this way a perfect footer could be generated.

Something similar to the fixation are those navigations, banners or texts that, in the same way as the fixation, are positioned somewhere but move and remain fixed only when the desired position is reached, for example the upper part. They are also known as sticky.

```
<h1 class="sticky-bottom"> fixed and sticky text below </h1>
```

```
<h1 class="fixed-top"> fixed and sticky text above
</h1>
```

Changing the color:

Let's see the default colors that bootstrap gives us. For colors, they are not named by default as red, yellow, or green. Rather, they have been assigned a class that represents a state. For example a red color can be a state of danger. In this way, any label that uses a color hazard type class will appear red, whether text or background. This is very useful for when we are creating applications and we want to mark the status or the type of text.

Let's see some examples of text with color and then a background also with color. Of course you can resort to making combinations, such as a background with one color and text of another color (see the last example in this list of examples). Clarification, although in this example I use a brand tag of type **<h1>**, remember that the tag can be of any type, for example a paragraph **<p>**.

<h1 class="texto-primary"> light blue text </h1>

<h1 class="text-success"> green text </h1>

<h1 class="text-info"> water green text </h1>

<h1 class="text-warning"> yellow text </h1>

<h1 class="text-success"> green text </h1>

<h1 class="text-danger"> red text </h1>

```
<h1 class="text-dark"> dark color text </h1>
```

```
<h1 class="text-white"> white text </h1>
```

```
<h1 class="invisible"> invisible color text </h1>
```

```
<h1 class="bg-info"> the background of the text is
aqua green </h1>
```

```
<h1 class="bg-primary"> in this case the background
is light blue </h1>
```

```
<h1 class="bg-dark text-white"> white text with dark
background </h1>
```

Margom & padding:

When we talk about spacing we refer to the **margin** and **padding** of the elements. It is worth clarifying that this class can be used in any tag of html. We will refer to the margins with the letter m and the padding with the letter **p**.

Then you must put a second letter that tells us what type of margin or padding we refer to.

T	Top	Top
B	Bottom	Bottom
L	Left	Left
R	Right	Right
X	Both X	Both Left & Right
Y	Both Y	Both Top & Bottom
Empty		The 4 R,L,T y B

And finally a third character, a number.

0	No margin or padding
1	Space 0.25
2	Space 0.5
3	Space 1
4	Space 1.5
5	Space 3
Auto	Automatic Margin (Only for margin)

Let's see an example with a type mark **<p>**.

```
<p class="mx-2"> Testing both margins with margin
0.5</p>
```

Finally we see in image 7 an example of padding where it leaves a space of 3 at the top, that is **pt-5**

```
<h1 class="bg-success pt-5">hello world</h1>
```

We can also say the width and / or height that a class will occupy. In the previous example we will add **w-25**, which indicates that this object will have a size that only occupies **25%** of the screen.

```
<h1 class="bg-success pt-5 w-25">hello world</h1>
```

Of course this number w can vary up to **100%**. In the same way, if we wanted to mark a high percentage, instead of using **w**, we would use **h**.

```
<h1 class="bg-success pt-5 h-25">hello world</h1>
```

Buttons:

The html mark to create a button is **<button>**, Inside is usually the type of button **type="subit" o type="reset"**, as to mention an example. Well, with bootstrap, we can also change its appearance or color with a class.

We already saw the colors in the texts before, well, this is something similar. The class is **class="btn"** and the color is similar to the text but with the **btn** characters in front.

Ex: **class="btn btn-primary"**

<button class="btn btn-primary"> Button</button>

In the same way I will give an example with a Yellow color.

<button class="btn btn-warning"> Button </button>

There is another type of color that we have not seen before that simulates a hyperlink, that is, a link.

<button class="btn btn-link"> Button</button>

Since these bootstrap classes are just that, we can give any tag these classes, for example if a type mark **<a>** which is used for links, we put a bootstrap class of button type, having a similar behavior will give us a good gift of a link with the button behavior, we see an example.

```
<a class="btn btn-primary" href="#"> Our Link </a>
```

Another type of button class is one that has a colored line around it and no color inside. The list of colors is the same that we have been learning, but the outline prefix is added to the class. Let's see an example.

```
<button class="btn btn-outline-primary"> Button </button>
```

We can also change the size of the buttons. Let's see an example of a big button.

```
<button class="btn btn-primary btn-lg"> Button </button>
```

We also have them in their small size, **class="btn-sm"**.

But we also have a new type which is block type, which covers the whole screen. **Class="btn-block"**

```
<button class="btn btn-primary btn-block"> Button </button>
```

Finally let's see a button, of type **dropdown**. This is like creating a menu. We will give an example of creating a menu button with three options.

```html
<div class="dropdown">
  <button class="btn btn-primary" data-togle="dropdown">
   Drop down
  </button>
  <div class="dropdown-menu">
    <a href="#" class="dropdown-item">Item One</a>
    <a href="#" class="dropdown-item">Item Two</a>
    <a href="#" class="dropdown-item">Item Three</a>
  </div>
</div>
```

It is also possible to create a group of buttons that will help us to create a menu, either with horizontal alignment, with the class **btn-group** or vertical with **class="btn-group-vertical"**

Ex:

```
<div class="btn-group">
  <button class="btn btn-primary">One</button>
  <button class="btn btn-primary">Two</button>
  <button class="btn btn-primary">Three</button>
</div>
```

To all this we could create different submenus within them as we saw previously.

Icon Library:

Just as bootstrap gives us a cdn of styles. There is also a well-known website that presents us with a cdn of icons. This is **fontawesome.com**

In the same way that we had added the bootstrap cdn, we will copy the link from the fontawesome website and put it in our header.

```
<head>
 <link rel="stylesheet" href="https://...>
</head>
```

The link can be obtained by registering on the website.

Now let's see an example of how to put an icon on our buttons, using a small label **<i>**.

```
<button class="btn btn-primary">
 <i class="fa fa-user"></i>
  Button
</button>
```

Being class **fa** by **fontawesome** and **fa-user** the type of icon. We can see a list of the icons available on the fontawesome website.

This is an example of many other icons cdn that we can find on the web.

List Group:

As we have already seen, when I have a group of objects I can orient them both vertically, which is how it comes by default or horizontally.

First of all we have to name the classes that make the list groups possible and that is: **list-group** for the creation of the list group in **list-group-item** to add each of the items. Finally I will mention that for the following example, as we have also seen previously, it is possible to create a list group with a different screen size, sm, md, lg, xl and for this example we will use a small horizontal alignment.

Cras justo odio   Dapibus ac facilisis in   Morbi leo risus

Image 8

```
<ul class="list-group list-group-sm">
  <li class="list-group-item">Cras justo odio</li>
  <li class="list-group-item">Dapibus ac facilisis
in</li>
  <li class="list-group-item">Morbi leo risus</li>
</ul>
```

Finally, if we wanted to change the color of the item we could do it by adding the color at the end of the class

```
<li class="list-group-item-primary">Morbi leo
risus</li>
```

Class badge:

Let's see two examples of this style, which is usually used to show the number of messages.

```
<button type="button" class="btn btn-primary">
  Profile <span class="badge badge-light">9</span>
  <span class="sr-only">unread messages</span>
</button>
```

Image 9

In this image taken from the bootstrap website we can see a code example and what badges look like.

Let's look at a second example also from the bootstrap website.

Primary Secondary Success Danger Warning Info Light Dark

```
<span class="badge badge-primary">Primary</span>
<span class="badge badge-secondary">Secondary</span>
<span class="badge badge-success">Success</span>
<span class="badge badge-danger">Danger</span>
<span class="badge badge-warning">Warning</span>
<span class="badge badge-info">Info</span>
<span class="badge badge-light">Light</span>
<span class="badge badge-dark">Dark</span>
```

Image 10

If we wanted to change the type of badge for a more oval one we can use the class **badge-pill**

Ex: **badge badge-pill**

Animation:

Let's see another famous cdn, but this time it allows you to create animations for any object.
We can find this in its git repository:
https://daneden.github.io/animate.css/

We just have to click on the button **view on github** and there we will find the following link:
https://github.com/daneden/animate.css

As we have seen so far, you just have to add the link **link** within the header to be able to use the cdn.

```
<head>
  <link rel="stylesheet" href="animate.min.css" >
</head>
```

This is if we have already downloaded the .css, otherwise we can also link directly to the animated host.

```
<link rel="stylesheet"
href="https://cdnjs.cloudflare.com/ajax/libs/animate.
css/3.7.2/animate.min.css">
```

Suppose what we want is to animate a card so to the bootstrap **card** class we will add the **animate** classes
Let's see an example code

```
<div class="card animated fadeInDown">Morbi leo
risus</li>
```

Where animated indicates that animation will be used and xxx tells us the type of animation, which I simply choose from the dropdown on the main page of the animated cdn and press the animate button.

In the case of this example what you will do is make an animation when loading the page where the card faces from above moving to the final position.

Navigation Bars:

In my opinion the navigation bars or navbar are one of the most beautiful things that the stylized bootstrap format has. To better understand what we are talking about, we can see below an example in the image of what a navigation bar would be and the code necessary to generate it.

Image 11

```
<nav class="navbar navbar-expand-lg navbar-light bg-light">
  <a class="navbar-brand" href="#">Navbar</a>
  <button class="navbar-toggler" type="button" data-toggle="collapse" data-target="#navbarSupportedContent" aria-controls = "navbarSupportedContent" aria-expanded="false" aria-label="Toggle navigation">
    <span class="navbar-toggler-icon"></span>
  </button>

  <div class="collapse navbar-collapse" id="navbarSupportedContent">
    <ul class="navbar-nav mr-auto">
      <li class="nav-item active">
      <a class="nav-link" href="#">Home <span class="sr-only"> (current) </span></a>
      </li>
      <li class="nav-item">
      <a class="nav-link" href="#">Link</a>
```

```
    </li>
    <li class="nav-item dropdown">
     <a class="nav-link dropdown-toggle" href="#"
id="navbarDropdown" role="button" data-
toggle="dropdown" aria-haspopup="true" aria-
expanded="false">
       Dropdown
     </a>
     <div class="dropdown-menu" aria-
labelledby="navbarDropdown">
       <a class="dropdown-item" href="#">Action</a>
       <a class="dropdown-item" href="#">Another
action</a>
       <div class="dropdown-divider"></div>
       <a class="dropdown-item" href="#">Something
else here</a>
     </div>
    </li>
    <li class="nav-item">
     <a class="nav-link disabled" href="#" tabindex="-
1" aria-disabled="true">Disabled</a>
    </li>
   </ul>
   <form class="form-inline my-2 my-lg-0">
    <input class="form-control mr-sm-2" type="search"
placeholder="Search" aria-label="Search">
    <button class="btn btn-outline-success my-2 my-
sm-0" type="submit">Search</button>
   </form>
  </div>
</nav>
```

As we see in the line below, we have a class of type navbar and then as we saw in previous examples we can indicate the size, in this case its size is lg or long. Actually the class used is navbar-expand-lg which means that the navigation bar will be expanded when the screen gets bigger. That means that otherwise, that is, when the screen is medium or small, as is the case with cell phones, the navigation bar will contract, leaving the menu folded or collapsed with the typical three-line button that indicates that we can display or collapse a menu of options.

Finally, it shows us the type of color or theme that the navigation bar will have, in this case it is light, that is, clear. Another option could be dark.

```
<nav class="navbar navbar-expand-lg navbar-light bg-light">
```

Debajo, en la segunda linea podemos apreciar como aparece aquel que hace de titulo o de logo de la barra

```
<a class="navbar-brand" href="#">Navbar</a>
```

And as we can see, this class is used inside a <A> type tag, this is to be able to generate a link when it is pressed.

The next part to highlight is the one we see below which is the code necessary to arm the collapsible button mentioned above.

```
<button class="navbar-toggler" type="button" data-toggle="collapse" data-
```

```
target="#navbarSupportedContent" aria-controls =
"navbarSupportedContent" aria-expanded="false" aria-
label="Toggle navigation">
  <span class="navbar-toggler-icon"></span>
 </button>
```

We can also see how to add some menu items in the form of a hyperlink

```
    <a class="nav-link" href="#">Home <span
class="sr-only"> (current) </span></a>
```

Or we see it more clearly with the following code with the bootstrap-specific **nav-item** class to create an item. With its corresponding **nav-link**

```
  <li class="nav-item">
   <a class="nav-link" href="#">Link</a>
  </li>
```

Below we see what is the code necessary to create that drop or drop-down that appears in the navigation bar with the arrow icon below.

```
    <li class="nav-item dropdown">
     <a class="nav-link dropdown-toggle" href="#"
id="navbarDropdown" role="button" data-
toggle="dropdown" aria-haspopup="true" aria-
expanded="false">
       Dropdown
     </a>
     <div class="dropdown-menu" aria-
labelledby="navbarDropdown">
```

```
    <a class="dropdown-item" href="#">Action</a>
    <a class="dropdown-item" href="#">Another
action</a>
      <div class="dropdown-divider"></div>
    <a class="dropdown-item" href="#">Something
else here</a>
    </div>
  </li>
```

And then the code needed to create the disabled button (disable)

```
  <li class="nav-item">
   <a class="nav-link disabled" href="#" tabindex="-
1" aria-disabled="true">Disabled</a>
  </li>
```

Finally the search form

```
  <form class="form-inline my-2 my-lg-0">
   <input class="form-control mr-sm-2" type="search"
placeholder="Search" aria-label="Search">
    <button class="btn btn-outline-success my-2 my-
sm-0" type="submit">Search</button>
  </form>
```

We see that this search form has a button of type btn btn-outline-success that will in turn submit

To finish with this example we should note that the sample code at the beginning has an html tag of type

<nav> and it closes with a </nav>. That allow the assembly of the navigation bar

```
<nav class="navbar navbar-expand-lg navbar-light bg-light">
.
.
.
</nav>
```

Now let's see another piece of example code as shown in image 12 to see how to add a logo to our bar

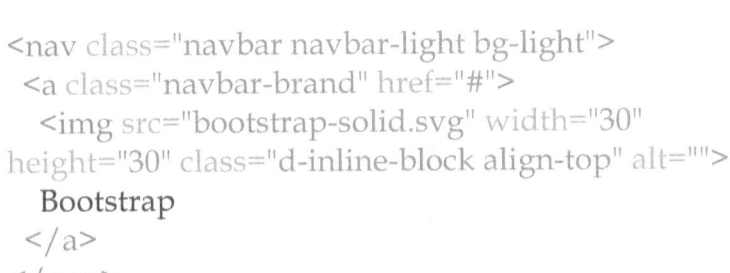

Image 12

```
<nav class="navbar navbar-light bg-light">
  <a class="navbar-brand" href="#">
    <img src="bootstrap-solid.svg" width="30" height="30" class="d-inline-block align-top" alt="">
    Bootstrap
  </a>
</nav>
```

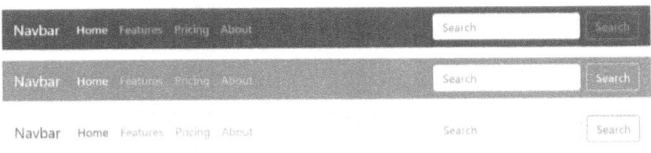

Image 13

In this last image we can see an example of different themes or schemes with different colors. Let's look at some code on this.

```
<nav class="navbar navbar-dark bg-dark">
  <!-- Navbar content -->
</nav>

<nav class="navbar navbar-dark bg-primary">
  <!-- Navbar content -->
</nav>

<nav class="navbar navbar-light" style="background-color: #e3f2fd;">
  <!-- Navbar content -->
</nav>
```

Finally its positioning. Below we will see three different codes. One to fix the bar at the top, the other to fix it at the bottom and finally a sticky that is fixed when you scroll the web page or application.

```
<nav class="navbar fixed-top navbar-light bg-light">
  <a class="navbar-brand" href="#">Fixed top</a>
</nav>

<nav class="navbar fixed-bottom navbar-light bg-light">
  <a class="navbar-brand" href="#">Fixed bottom</a>
</nav>
```

```
<nav class="navbar sticky-top navbar-light bg-light">
  <a class="navbar-brand" href="#">Sticky top</a>
</nav>
```

Another option that can be exploited is to use these collapsible buttons and enter certain information that would not necessarily have to have items or links. What could if we wanted. Let's see in figure 14 and 15 first collapsed, then without collapsing and to finish the example code provided by the bootstrap page.

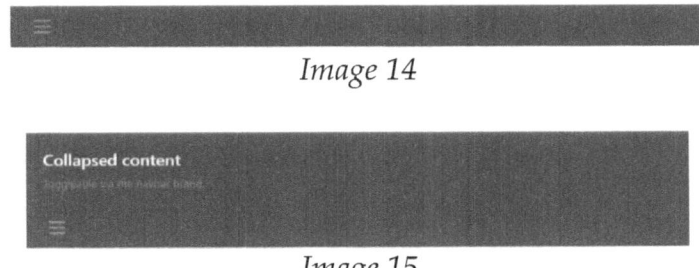

Image 14

Image 15

```
<div class="pos-f-t">
  <div class="collapse"
id="navbarToggleExternalContent">
    <div class="bg-dark p-4">
      <h5 class="text-white h4">Collapsed content</h5>
      <span class="text-muted">Toggleable via the
navbar brand.</span>
    </div>
  </div>
```

```
<nav class="navbar navbar-dark bg-dark">
  <button class="navbar-toggler" type="button" data-
toggle="collapse" data-
target="#navbarToggleExternalContent" aria-
controls="navbarToggleExternalContent" aria-
expanded="false" aria-label="Toggle navigation">
    <span class="navbar-toggler-icon"></span>
  </button>
</nav>
</div>
```

Alerts:

And Now as we see in image 16, it is the turn of alerts. We will see two examples, the example in image 16 and the one in image 17, which are also alerts, but they have hyperlinks inside. In this way the hyperlink style is stylized to match the alert style. And in the example in image 18, we will also see a simple alert. But this time it will have a small icon on the right in the form of a cross, which is in charge of closing that **alert**.

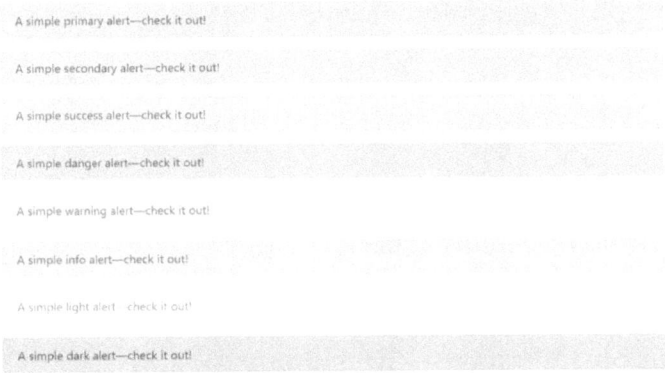

Image 16

```
<div class="alert alert-primary" role="alert">
A simple primary alert—check it out!
</div>
<div class="alert alert-secondary" role="alert">
A simple secondary alert—check it out!
</div>
<div class="alert alert-success" role="alert">
A simple success alert—check it out!
</div>
<div class="alert alert-danger" role="alert">
A simple danger alert—check it out!
</div>
<div class="alert alert-warning" role="alert">
A simple warning alert—check it out!
</div>
<div class="alert alert-info" role="alert">
A simple info alert—check it out!
</div>
<div class="alert alert-light" role="alert">
A simple light alert—check it out!
</div>
<div class="alert alert-dark" role="alert">
A simple dark alert—check it out!
</div>
```

As we see the code is very simple. Only the alert class and its color, as examples from previous classes. In this first code for example alert-primary. We also see that the role tag in this case would be **Alert**

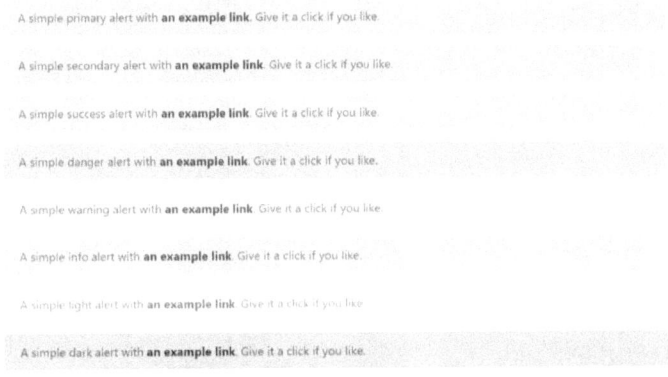

A simple primary alert with **an example link**. Give it a click if you like

A simple secondary alert with **an example link**. Give it a click if you like

A simple success alert with **an example link**. Give it a click if you like

A simple danger alert with **an example link**. Give it a click if you like.

A simple warning alert with **an example link**. Give it a click if you like

A simple info alert with **an example link**. Give it a click if you like

A simple light alert with **an example link**. Give it a click if you like

A simple dark alert with **an example link**. Give it a click if you like.

Image 17

```
<div class="alert alert-primary" role="alert">
A simple primary alert with <a href="#" class="alert-link">an example link</a>. Give it a click if you like.
</div>
<div class="alert alert-secondary" role="alert">
A simple secondary alert with <a href="#" class="alert-link">an example link</a>. Give it a click if you like.
</div>
<div class="alert alert-success" role="alert">
A simple success alert with <a href="#" class="alert-link">an example link</a>. Give it a click if you like.
</div>
<div class="alert alert-danger" role="alert">
A simple danger alert with <a href="#" class="alert-link">an example link</a>. Give it a click if you like.
</div>
<div class="alert alert-warning" role="alert">
A simple warning alert with <a href="#" class="alert-link">an example link</a>. Give it a click if you like.
```

```
</div>
<div class="alert alert-info" role="alert">
  A simple info alert with <a href="#" class="alert-
link">an example link</a>. Give it a click if you like.
</div>
<div class="alert alert-light" role="alert">
  A simple light alert with <a href="#" class="alert-
link">an example link</a>. Give it a click if you like.
</div>
<div class="alert alert-dark" role="alert">
  A simple dark alert with <a href="#" class="alert-
link">an example link</a>. Give it a click if you like.
</div>
```

As we see in the example the code is very simple.

```
<div class="alert alert-primary" role="alert">
  A simple primary alert with <a href="#" class="alert-
link">an example link</a>. Give it a click if you like.
</div>
```

It is only a **<div>** with an alert class as we have seen, first it takes the class type and then the color. In this case **alert-primary**. But we also have the **alert-link** class which is to put our hyperlink.

In the last case, let's see image 18 that shows us how to put that button that allows us to close the alert as we had previously mentioned.

Holy guacamole! You should check in on some of those fields below.   ×

Image 18

```
<div class="alert alert-warning alert-dismissible fade
show" role="alert">
  <strong>Holy guacamole!</strong> You should
check in on some of those fields below.
  <button type="button" class="close" data-
dismiss="alert" aria-label="Close">
    <span aria-hidden="true">&times;</span>
  </button>
</div>
```

Progress bars:

Let's see now some examples of progress bar.

Image 19

Now let's see the html code necessary to generate this progress bar with its label, in this case 25%.

```
<div class="progress">
 <div class="progress-bar" role="progressbar"
style="width: 25%;" aria-valuenow="25" aria-
valuemin="0" aria-valuemax="100">25%</div>
</div>
```

As you can see it is a short code. At this point in the book it is not necessary to explain the names of the classes, it is only necessary in this case to point out that we have 3 number 25, the first will be the width of the blue bar, then we have the current value, see that it has a minimum value and maximum and finally before the div, we have 25% which is the text that appears in the example.

In *image 19* we can see another example, but this time, changing the background color of the progress bar.

Image 20

```
<div class="progress">
```

```
  <div class="progress-bar bg-success"
role="progressbar" style="width: 25%" aria-
valuenow="25" aria-valuemin="0" aria-
valuemax="100"></div>
</div>
<div class="progress">
  <div class="progress-bar bg-info" role="progressbar"
style="width: 50%" aria-valuenow="50" aria-
valuemin="0" aria-valuemax="100"></div>
</div>
<div class="progress">
  <div class="progress-bar bg-warning"
role="progressbar" style="width: 75%" aria-
valuenow="75" aria-valuemin="0" aria-
valuemax="100"></div>
</div>
<div class="progress">
  <div class="progress-bar bg-danger"
role="progressbar" style="width: 100%" aria-
valuenow="100" aria-valuemin="0" aria-
valuemax="100"></div>
</div>
```

As I said earlier at this point, the examples are easy to understand, so the explanations are superfluous. This also makes it easier to enter the official bootstrap page and understand most of the examples that are presented there.

The official bootstrap site has a small search bar where one can put the text to search. As in this case "**progress**" and it will give us as results different examples of the different classes. This will help the reader to see the rest of the classes, perhaps new or existing that escape this book.

We see another example, but this time the one of a bar that contains a particular style and separate an animation. We can see it in the next image and the next code.

Image 21

```
<div class="progress">
 <div class="progress-bar progress-bar-striped
progress-bar-animated" role="progressbar" aria-
valuenow="75" aria-valuemin="0" aria-valuemax="100"
style="width: 75%"></div>
</div>
```

But this time I recommend you go take a look at the codes and examples of the bars that are presented on the official bootstrap page. I leave you a link to the progress bars:

https://getbootstrap.com/docs/4.3/components/prog ress

As you will see the examples are already easy to understand, and you can clearly see that on a topic seen in the book, on the pages you have abundant information, different types and their example codes.

It is missing a few to finish:

We are already finishing learning the basic concepts, we just need to see some important or nice classes and at the end of the book we will see an example of a website created with bootstrap. As they say, a real life example.

Next we will see: The cards (card), Carousel, Forms (forms), Jumbotron, Modal Windows (modal), Popovers, Spinners, Toasts, Embeds, Shadows, and finally we will see the aforementioned example of real life.

Las tarjetas (card):

The cards are neither more nor less than containers. Or at least that's how bootstrap defines them. These containers consist of a header and a body. Of course, as they are all or better said, most bootstrap classes tend to have the same styles, that is why lists or hyperlinks are created to be able to use within this card class. Let's see some examples (*Image 22*) that we will also interpret from the official bootstrap website.

Image 22

```html
<div class="card" style="width: 18rem;">
  <img src="..." class="card-img-top" alt="...">
  <div class="card-body">
    <h5 class="card-title">Card title</h5>
    <p class="card-text">Some quick example text to
build on the card title and make up the bulk of the
card's content.</p>
    <a href="#" class="btn btn-primary">Go
somewhere</a>
  </div>
</div>
```

In this code it is clear that the class is called **card** and in the style we are clearly seeing the width, we also see that it has an image that is positioned at the top and a body or **card-body** and we see that it uses a style for the title called **card-text** and although it is easy to deduce let's see the last two styles seen in this example, which are **card-text** for inside text and **btn btn-primary** which is neither more nor less than a button as we had clearly seen earlier in this book.

Let's see what are the classes for the links.

```html
<a href="#" class="card-link">Card link</a>
<a href="#" class="card-link">Another link</a>
```

And let's also look at the class to use the lists.

```html
<ul class="list-group list-group-flush">
  <li class="list-group-item">Cras justo odio</li>
```

```
   <li class="list-group-item">Dapibus ac facilisis
in</li>
   <li class="list-group-item">Vestibulum at eros</li>
   </ul>
```

And in the next example of Image 23, we will see to finish with the topic cards an example that uses not only the header and the body, but also the footer.

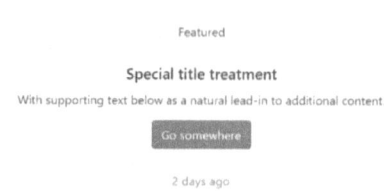

Image 23

```
<div class="card text-center">
 <div class="card-header">
  Featured
 </div>
 <div class="card-body">
  <h5 class="card-title">Special title treatment</h5>
  <p class="card-text">With supporting text below as a
natural lead-in to additional content.</p>
  <a href="#" class="btn btn-primary">Go
somewhere</a>
 </div>
 <div class="card-footer text-muted">
  2 days ago
 </div>
</div>
```

I think the code is self explanatory. I recommend viewing the subject of card lineups and background colors at the following web address:

https://getbootstrap.com/docs/4.4/components/card/

Carousel:

The carousel is easier to identify by an image, and we will see it *in Image 24*, it is the typical heading that wordpress blogs usually have where it contains several images or texts or containers that slide automatically..

Image 24

```
<div id="carouselExampleControls" class="carousel
slide" data-ride="carousel">
 <div class="carousel-inner">
  <div class="carousel-item active">
   <img src="..." class="d-block w-100" alt="...">
  </div>
  <div class="carousel-item">
   <img src="..." class="d-block w-100" alt="...">
  </div>
  <div class="carousel-item">
   <img src="..." class="d-block w-100" alt="...">
  </div>
 </div>
```

```
  <a class="carousel-control-prev"
href="#carouselExampleControls" role="button" data-
slide="prev">
    <span class="carousel-control-prev-icon" aria-
hidden="true"></span>
    <span class="sr-only">Previous</span>
  </a>
  <a class="carousel-control-next"
href="#carouselExampleControls" role="button" data-
slide="next">
    <span class="carousel-control-next-icon" aria-
hidden="true"></span>
    <span class="sr-only">Next</span>
  </a>
</div>
```

In this code, we clearly see that the carousel is divided into items, one of them active, on the other hand it also has a previous control and another next.

Please see the official bootstrap website to find more examples and style that can be generated with this nice class.

Forms:

Let's see a simple example of a form in Image 25 with its corresponding example code below, although in the final part of this book we will give a practical example called Real-life example, where we will return to the concept of the use of forms, but this time framed in some kind of container to format it.

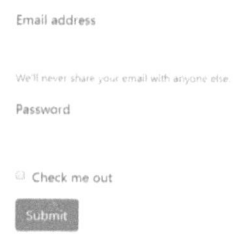

Email address

We'll never share your email with anyone else.

Password

Check me out

Submit

Image 25

```
<form>
 <div class="form-group">
  <label for="exampleInputEmail1">Email
address</label>
  <input type="email" class="form-control"
id="exampleInputEmail1" aria-
describedby="emailHelp">
  <small id="emailHelp" class="form-text text-
muted">We'll never share your email with anyone
else.</small>
 </div>
 <div class="form-group">
  <label
for="exampleInputPassword1">Password</label>
  <input type="password" class="form-control"
id="exampleInputPassword1">
 </div>
 <div class="form-group form-check">
  <input type="checkbox" class="form-check-input"
id="exampleCheck1">
  <label class="form-check-label"
for="exampleCheck1">Check me out</label>
 </div>
 <button type="submit" class="btn btn-
primary">Submit</button>
</form>
```

If you have a little understanding of html and form handling, this code should be self explanatory. If not, I recommend you do a little research on the use of forms, which is quite widely used, but which escapes this book since it understands a slightly more advanced use of html.

I also recommend looking for information on the official bootstrap site about how to stylize the different elements that make up forms.

Jumbotron:

As in the case of carousel, it is easier to identify a Jumbotron if we see what it is in image 26. Although we can anticipate that it is another type of container, such as cards.

Image 26

Do not be fooled by the size of the image, this jumbotron container is quite large and I want to clarify that you can also put it inside a **container**, using the different **div** tags and container classes, this would be used to align or resize it . Now here below we will see the code that makes this example possible.

```
<div class="jumbotron">
  <h1 class="display-4">Hello, world!</h1>
  <p class="lead">This is a simple hero unit, a simple jumbotron-style component for calling extra attention to featured content or information.</p>
  <hr class="my-4">
  <p>It uses utility classes for typography and spacing to space content out within the larger container.</p>
```

```
 <a class="btn btn-primary btn-lg" href="#"
role="button">Learn more</a>
</div>
```

Modals:

They are those windows that open within the browser window that show us some indication. In order to carry out this exercise we must first create a button that will be the culprit of the event that triggered our modal window. Let's see *Image 27* with its corresponding code, that when pressing the general button the example of *Image 28* also with its corresponding code.

Image 27

```
<!-- Button trigger modal -->
<button type="button" class="btn btn-primary" data-toggle="modal" data-target="#exampleModal">
  Launch demo modal
</button>
```

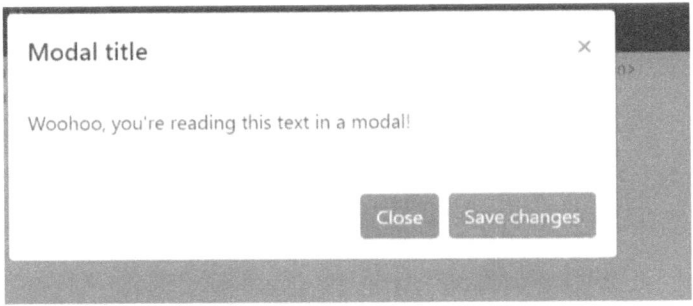

Image 28

We can clearly see how the rest of the page is covered by a transparent black color, which indicates that it is currently disabled, waiting for an action to be generated in the modal window.

We can also see that as an example we have in the upper right corner an x that serves as a close button and also has a button that says **close** that will also serve us for the same action. In this example the other button has the text **Save changes** that in reality it will not do anything since an action of this type was not executed since this is only an example.

```
<!-- Modal -->
<div class="modal fade" id="exampleModal"
tabindex="-1" role="dialog" aria-
labelledby="exampleModalLabel" aria-hidden="true">
  <div class="modal-dialog" role="document">
    <div class="modal-content">
      <div class="modal-header">
        <h5 class="modal-title"
id="exampleModalLabel">Modal title</h5>
        <button type="button" class="close" data-
dismiss="modal" aria-label="Close">
          <span aria-hidden="true">&times;</span>
        </button>
      </div>
      <div class="modal-body">
        ...
      </div>
      <div class="modal-footer">
```

```
    <button type="button" class="btn btn-secondary"
data-dismiss="modal">Close</button>
    <button type="button" class="btn btn-
primary">Save changes</button>
   </div>
  </div>
 </div>
</div>
```

As we see the code is easy to understand and read.

Popovers:

We will see clearly from what *Image 29* shows us that a **Pop Over** appears with more information when the button is pressed. This is clearly illustrated in *Image 30*.

Image 29

Image 30

Let's look at the code that makes this possible.

```
<button type="button" class="btn btn-lg btn-danger"
data-toggle="popover" title="Popover title" data-
content="And here's some amazing content. It's very
engaging. Right?">Click to toggle popover</button>
```

Spinners:

I encourage the reader to enter:
https://getbootstrap.com/docs/4.4/components/spinners/
In order to appreciate the different types of Spinners (rotating icons) and the various examples of how to generate them, we will see here a code that changes different colors and also Image 31 that shows us the appearance of these spinners

Image 31

```
<div class="spinner-border text-primary"
role="status">
  <span class="sr-only">Loading...</span>
</div>
<div class="spinner-border text-secondary"
role="status">
  <span class="sr-only">Loading...</span>
</div>
<div class="spinner-border text-success" role="status">
  <span class="sr-only">Loading...</span>
</div>
<div class="spinner-border text-danger" role="status">
  <span class="sr-only">Loading...</span>
</div>
<div class="spinner-border text-warning"
role="status">
  <span class="sr-only">Loading...</span>
</div>
```

```
<div class="spinner-border text-info" role="status">
  <span class="sr-only">Loading...</span>
</div>
<div class="spinner-border text-light" role="status">
  <span class="sr-only">Loading...</span>
</div>
<div class="spinner-border text-dark" role="status">
  <span class="sr-only">Loading...</span>
</div>
```

Toasts:

In this example we will not see the simplest one that would be to generate a single one, we will see one called stack, where several are accumulating. In this case two and it is more practical since we can see what happens when they are closed.

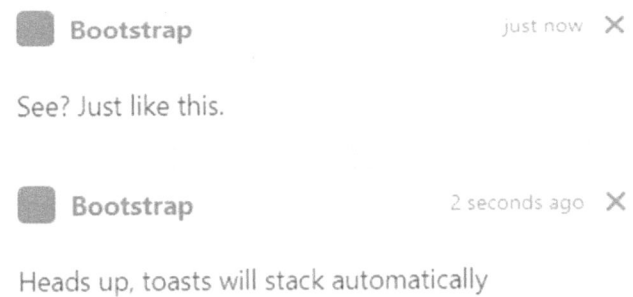

Image 32

```html
<div class="toast" role="alert" aria-live="assertive" aria-atomic="true">
  <div class="toast-header">
    <img src="..." class="rounded mr-2" alt="...">
    <strong class="mr-auto">Bootstrap</strong>
    <small class="text-muted">just now</small>
    <button type="button" class="ml-2 mb-1 close" data-dismiss="toast" aria-label="Close">
      <span aria-hidden="true">&times;</span>
    </button>
  </div>
  <div class="toast-body">
```

See? Just like this.
```
   </div>
</div>
```

```
<div class="toast" role="alert" aria-live="assertive" aria-atomic="true">
  <div class="toast-header">
    <img src="..." class="rounded mr-2" alt="...">
    <strong class="mr-auto">Bootstrap</strong>
    <small class="text-muted">2 seconds ago</small>
    <button type="button" class="ml-2 mb-1 close" data-dismiss="toast" aria-label="Close">
      <span aria-hidden="true">&times;</span>
    </button>
  </div>
  <div class="toast-body">
    Heads up, toasts will stack automatically
  </div>
</div>
```

We see clearly how the code is divided into two **toast** alerts, which we must mention that they are nice and even fun.

Embeds:

Embedded objects, such as videos or audios, are the first last topic we will be looking at, before moving on to what we call a **Real Life Example**.

```
<div class="embed-responsive embed-responsive-16by9">
  <iframe class="embed-responsive-item" src="https://www.youtube.com/embed/......" allowfullscreen></iframe>
</div>
```

Shadows:

No shadow

Small shadow

Regular shadow

Larger shadow

Image 33

<div class="shadow-none p-3 mb-5 bg-light rounded">No shadow</div>
<div class="shadow-sm p-3 mb-5 bg-white rounded">Small shadow</div>
<div class="shadow p-3 mb-5 bg-white rounded">Regular shadow</div>
<div class="shadow-lg p-3 mb-5 bg-white rounded">Larger shadow</div>

To end:

Well, and with this we have reached the end of the list of styles that you select to teach them, as I always mention if they enter the official website they will be able to find many more examples and many more styles, but having finished this book, the reader is trained to fully understand the official bootstrap site.

Real life example:

```html
<!DOCTYPE html>
<html lang="en">
  <head>
<meta name="keywords" content=" Bleach, detergent,
cleaning products, cleaning ">
    <meta charset="utf-8">
    <meta name="viewport" content="width=device-
width, initial-scale=1, shrink-to-fit=no">
    <title> Cleaning products </title>
    <link rel="stylesheet"
href="https://stackpath.bootstrapcdn.com/bootstrap/
4.3.1/css/bootstrap.min.css" integrity="sha384-
ggOyR0iXCbMQv3Xipma34MD+dH/1fQ784/j6cY/iJT
QUOhcWr7x9JvoRxT2MZw1T"
crossorigin="anonymous">

<script data-ad-client="ca-pub-000000000000" async
src="https://pagead2.googlesyndication.com/pagead/
js/adsbygoogle.js"></script>

  </head>
    <img src="./up.jpg" class="img-fluid mx-auto d-
block">
<div class="container" style="background:transparent
url('./background.jpg') no-repeat center center /cover"
>
<body style="background-color:black;">

<nav class="navbar navbar-expand-lg navbar-dark bg-
dark sticky-top">
```

```
<a class="navbar-brand" href="#"> Cleaning Items for
Sale </a>
<button class="navbar-toggler" type="button" data-
toggle="collapse" data-
target="#navbarNavAltMarkup" aria-
controls="navbarNavAltMarkup" aria-
expanded="false" aria-label="Toggle navigation">
  <span class="navbar-toggler-icon"></span>
</button>
<div          class="collapse          navbar-collapse"
id="navbarNavAltMarkup">
  <div class="navbar-nav">
  <a class="nav-item nav-link active"
href="index.htm">Home <span class="sr-
only">(current)</span></a>
  <a class="nav-item nav-link" href="articles.htm">
Catalog of Articles </a>
  <a class="nav-item nav-link" href="sales.htm">
Selling points </a>
  <a class="nav-item nav-link"
href="contaco.htm">Contact Us</a>
  </div>
  </div>
</nav>

  <h2 class="text-center text-white-50"> Welcome to
<strong> cleaningarticlesexample.com
</strong></h2>
      <br>
      <p class="text-justify mx-4 text-light"> You
have reached the most complete site for the sale of
cleaning products online.</p>
      <br>
```

```
                <p class="text-center text-danger"><strong>
Please note that all our products are guaranteed
</strong></p>


                <p class="text-center text-white-50"> Click
on the desired product </p>
                <a class="text-center nav-item nav-link text-
danger" href="lavandina.htm">Lavandinas</a>
            <a class="text-center nav-item nav-link text-
danger" href="detergents.htm"> detergents </a>
                <a class="text-center nav-item nav-link text-
danger" href="desinfectants.htm"> Disinfectants </a>
                <p class="text-center invisible"> detergents,
lavandinas, soaps, cloth rags, cleaning products,
disinfectants </p>
                <br>
<hr>
<p class="text-justify text-muted mx-3">
<strong> Terms and conditions of the service
</strong><br>
We categorically and definitively deny any contact with
minors under 18 years of age. I will use the services and
/ or products. Using any of the services or products
will be considered acceptance of these policies and
terms..

</p>
<br>


<a class="text-center nav-item nav-link text-white"
href="privacy.htm"> Privacy </a>
```

```html
<a class="fixed-bottom text-info ml-5"
href="cookies.htm"><strong> Information on the use
of cookies </strong></a>

    <script src="https://code.jquery.com/jquery-
3.3.1.slim.min.js" integrity="sha384-
q8i/X+965DzO0rT7abK41JStQIAqVgRVzpbzo5smXKp
4YfRvH+8abtTE1Pi6jizo"
crossorigin="anonymous"></script>
    <script
src="https://cdnjs.cloudflare.com/ajax/libs/popper.js
/1.14.7/umd/popper.min.js" integrity="sha384-
UO2eT0CpHqdSJQ6hJty5KVphtPhzWj9WO1clHTMGa
3JDZwrnQq4sF86dIHNDz0W1"
crossorigin="anonymous"></script>
    <script
src="https://stackpath.bootstrapcdn.com/bootstrap/4.
3.1/js/bootstrap.min.js" integrity="sha384-
JjSmVgyd0p3pXB1rRibZUAYoIy6OrQ6VrjIEaFf/nJGz
IxFDsf4x0xIM+B07jRM"
crossorigin="anonymous"></script>
  </body>
</div>
</html>
```

Code analysis:

Do a quick read and scan of the code, and ask yourself what it is about. If you said that it looks like a website, part of a website dedicated to the sale of cleaning products, we are on the right track.

Now let's start analyzing each fragment.

```
<!DOCTYPE html>
<html lang="en">
  <head>
```

We head with the document format which in this case is **html** and we say that it is the language of the content will be mostly in **English** and then we open the tag **<head>** which is where we will put the header data.

```
<meta name="keywords" content=" Bleach, detergent,
cleaning products, cleaning">
  <meta charset="utf-8">
  <meta name="viewport" content="width=device-
width, initial-scale=1, shrink-to-fit=no">
  <title> Cleaning products </title>
```

Here, in this part of the code and within the heading, we see the **keyword** tags that are used to put the keywords, what does it mean ?, that when the search engine indexes our site (for example google) it will see that our website wants to be found with these keywords, in this example: Bleach, detergent, cleaning products, cleaning.

Another tag that we see, that comes just below is **charset** that its translation is character set, in this case the character set that was chosen is **utf-8** this is so that accents, ñ and other special characters are fine represented on the website.

We also have the **viewport** which is the one that indicates the scale of the device.

And finally **<title>** that is used to show the title of the website, which will be shown in the title bar of the browser window.

Well so far things don't make much difference with other site that doesn't use bootstrap. But it was worth explaining this a little above, for that reader who was not entirely clear on the concepts. And for those who already knew them to review.

```
<link rel="stylesheet"
href="https://stackpath.bootstrapcdn.com/bootstrap/
4.3.1/css/bootstrap.min.css" integrity="sha384-
ggOyR0iXCbMQv3Xipma34MD+dH/1fQ784/j6cY/iJT
QUOhcWr7x9JvoRxT2MZw1T"
crossorigin="anonymous">
```

This line headed by **link** is the one we had pointed out at the beginning of the book, which allows us to have access to the bootstrap codes and styles.

```
<script data-ad-client="ca-pub-000000000000" async
src="https://pagead2.googlesyndication.com/pagead/
js/adsbygoogle.js"></script>
```

```
</head>
```

And here is a good place to put the code provided by google ads for automatic ads within our site. And then finish with the header with **</head>**.

```
<img src="./up.jpg" class="img-fluid mx-auto d-block">
```

With this line of code we put an image as a banner at the top of the page, whose image file is called **up.jpg** and is located in the root directory of our website.

```
<div class="container" style="background:transparent url('./background.jpg') no-repeat center center /cover">
<body style="background-color:black;">
```

In this other part, what we do is say that the background image that will appear on our website is./background.jpg and that the background color of the website that will be below the image will be black.

```
<nav class="navbar navbar-expand-lg navbar-dark bg-dark sticky-top">
  <a class="navbar-brand" href="#"> Cleaning Items for Sale </a>
  <button class="navbar-toggler" type="button" data-toggle="collapse" data-target="#navbarNavAltMarkup" aria-controls="navbarNavAltMarkup" aria-expanded="false" aria-label="Toggle navigation">
```

```
<span class="navbar-toggler-icon"></span>
</button>
<div class="collapse navbar-collapse"
id="navbarNavAltMarkup">
<div class="navbar-nav">
<a class="nav-item nav-link active"
href="index.htm">Home <span class="sr-
only">(current)</span></a>
<a class="nav-item nav-link" href="articles.htm">
Catalog of Articles </a>
<a class="nav-item nav-link" href=" sales.htm">
Selling points </a>
<a class="nav-item nav-link"
href="contact.htm">Contact Us</a>
</div>
</div>
</nav>
```

Clearly in this text block is where we create the menu
or navigation bar, with its link and its corresponding
links, such as **contact** with **contact.htm** Let's also see
that we put icons and some other peculiarities that we
had seen when seeing the **navbar**

```
<h2 class="text-center text-white-50"> Welcome to
<strong> cleaningarticlesexample.com
</strong></h2>
    <br>
        <p class="text-justify mx-4 text-light"> You
have reached the most complete site for the sale of
cleaning products online.</p>
        <br>
```

<p class="text-center text-danger"><strong>
Please note that all our products are guaranteed
</strong></p>

<p class="text-center text-white-50"> Click
on the desired product </p>
<a class="text-center nav-item nav-link text-danger" href="lavandina.htm">Lavandinas</a>
<a class="text-center nav-item nav-link text-danger" href="detergente.htm"> detergents </a>
<a class="text-center nav-item nav-link text-danger" href="desinfectantes.htm"> Disinfectants </a>
<p class="text-center invisible"> detergents,
lavandinas, soaps, cloth rags, cleaning products,
disinfectants </p>

<hr>
<p class="text-justify text-muted mx-3">
<strong> Terms and conditions of the service
</strong>
We categorically and definitively deny any contact with
minors under 18 years of age. I will use the services and
/ or products. Using any of the services or products
will be considered acceptance of these policies and
terms..

</p>

<a class="text-center nav-item nav-link text-white"
href=" Privacy.htm"> Privacy </a>

In all this text we have the content of the page itself. It
starts with an h2-type title that says Welcome to ... with

strong tags to highlight the site name and then, below, some texts with hyperlinks to the content. We even have invisible type texts that will be used, also for indexing by search engines, but which will not be visible on our website.

Almost at the end we find the conditions of use of the website.

And to finish a link that sends us to the page where the site's privacy policies are clarified.

```
<a class="fixed-bottom text-info ml-5"
href="cookies.htm"><strong> Information on the use
of cookies </strong></a>
```

This is a hyperlink that remains floating as you scroll the page that indicates that we click if we want to access the page that contains the description of the use of cookies, as requested by the policies of some regions, such as the European Union.

```
<script src="https://code.jquery.com/jquery-
3.3.1.slim.min.js" integrity="sha384-
q8i/X+965DzO0rT7abK41JStQIAqVgRVzpbzo5smXKp
4YfRvH+8abtTE1Pi6jizo"
crossorigin="anonymous"></script>
<script
src="https://cdnjs.cloudflare.com/ajax/libs/popper.js
/1.14.7/umd/popper.min.js" integrity="sha384-
UO2eT0CpHqdSJQ6hJty5KVphtPhzWj9WO1clHTMGa
3JDZwrnQq4sF86dIHNDz0W1"
crossorigin="anonymous"></script>
<script
src="https://stackpath.bootstrapcdn.com/bootstrap/4.
3.1/js/bootstrap.min.js" integrity="sha384-
JjSmVgyd0p3pXB1rRibZUAYoIIy6OrQ6VrjIEaFf/nJGz
IxFDsf4x0xIM+B07jRM"
crossorigin="anonymous"></script>
```

As we had said at the beginning of the book, we not only need to include the **link** tag in the header so that bootstrap can be used or rather the bootstrap styles, but it is also necessary to include the java scripts necessary for the behavior of the website. As it is well known, since java scripts take a little longer to load, it is advisable to put them just before closing **</body>** so that all the content of the site can be shown and finally the browser will have the opportunity to load the behavior of each object and each button, becoming almost imperceptible to the navigator.

```
</body>
</div>
</html>
```

We see in this final part, what is done is to close the body, that div of the beginning and also the html code.

We have reached the end of the book and I hope the reader has been able to get a good.

We recommend you enter:

www.whitetowerpublishing.com/code/bootstrap_01_en.htm

If you want to access the example code provided as a real life example.

Libros recomendados de la editorial

Computing:

Quantum Computing
Delphi - User Manual
Delphi - Beginners
Artificial intelligence
Linux - Beginners
PHP - User Manual
PHP - Beginners
Python - User Manual
Python - Beginners
WebGL - Babylon.JS

Languages:

Arabic - Beginners

Movies:
Direction of photography

You can access the complete catalog of books by
entering the publisher's website
www.whitetowerpublishing.com

ABOUT THE AUTHOR

Electronics Technician and Programmer Analyst.
Integral Film and Television Director, Director of
Photography. Writer, Screenwriter, Translator Spanish,
Portuguese, Italian, German, English.

E-Mail
cancinos@hotmail.com